101+
MEASURABLE IEP
GOALS & OBJECTIVES

for Developing Executive Functions

Every Child can Succeed!

CHRIS DE FEYTER, EdD

First edition

ISBN-13: 9781508703068

Cover Image by Humbert15, used under Creative Commons License.

This publication is not connected to or affiliated with the book *Smart but Scattered* by Dawson and Guare, published by The Guilford Press. This publication does not replace *Smart but Scattered*. In fact, the author highly recommends any educator to purchase *Smart but Scattered* through their favorite retailer.

Content

Page intentionally left blank

Introduction

Working with students who have diverse needs is a very interesting aspect of educating children. Doing well all that helps students achieve is a passion many educators share. Or at least that is what I have come to experience during my time in education as a consultant and teacher.

When a few years ago, a teacher contacted me about executive functions, I was thrilled about her call. She had read "Smart but Scattered" by Dawson and Guare and was wondering if I had any additional resources she could use with a number of her high needs students. We brainstormed for a while and came up with some interesting differentiated strategies and out-of-the-box ideas.

A few years later, after the release of the second edition of my book "800+ measurable IEP Goals and Objectives", I began to receive emails from readers who were wondering if any of the goals I had constructed in my book could fit with "executive functions". My initial answer however did not satisfy the majority of email writers, as I stated that any goal out of my book could somehow directly be connected to executive functions. One reader even suggested picking or creating goals and fitting them with some of the categories Dawson and Guare had used in their book. This reader had also attended a workshop on Smart but Scattered, and strongly believed fitting goals with "new scientific discoveries called executive functions" would be very helpful.

This book is exactly what the above teacher suggested. I have taken the 125 mostly used goals and objectives from my bestselling book "800+ measurable IEP Goals and Objectives" and arranged those according to 7 categories used by Dawson and Guare. Many goals would probably fit I multiple areas, but to keep it simple, I focused on the first category that came to mind.

Why did I only select 125 goals? I believe it is better to have a few very good goals than too many that really focus on a whole lot of nothing. Instead of creating new goals for students with similar needs, I recommend adjusting these goals to make then fit. More about this in the next section *How to Use this Book.*

Chris de Feyter

How to Use this Book

Method one: The *Lazy* Way

You could select goals from this book and use them as is, stating the area of focus (i.e.: sustaining focus and attention). Find a strategy or two and there you go: a **"good"** plan.

Positives: efficient use of time

Negatives: non-individualized plans for students.

Method two: The *Easy* Way

You could on the other hand select goals from this book, adjust a bit here and there, stating the area of focus (i.e.: sustaining focus and attention). Find a strategy or two and there you go: a **"better"** plan.

Method three: The *right* way

You should select a goal, and adjust to make it fit slightly above the current level of performance of student. Find one or two best-practice strategies, making sure these fit with the learning style of the student: a **"fine"** plan.

Example.

Justin is 9 years old, and is often feeling angry. It is difficult to determine antecedents. In a learning contract, Justin has agreed to learn replacement behaviors to manage his outbursts.

Verbatim Goal:

By June, Student will independently identify and demonstrate a list of 8 different strategies one may use when they are feeling angry or upset in class, with 85% accuracy in 4 out of 5 trials, as documented in Student's log.

Changed Goal:

By June, Student will independently identify and demonstrate a list of 3 different strategies he may use when he is feeling angry or upset in class, with 80% accuracy in 4 out of 5 trials, as documented in Student's log.

Individualized Goal:

By June, Student will independently identify and demonstrate 3 different strategies (counting to 5, deep breathing, asking for a break) he may use when he is feeling angry or upset in class, with 80% accuracy in 4 out of 5 trials, as documented in Student's log.

Developmentally appropriate

Selecting goals because the skill or routine fits with what other students of the same age do or master is a mistake made by many educators I have worked with. Rather than choosing age-appropriate goals, I recommend selecting a goal and making it developmentally appropriate.

Example

Let us look at Peter, a 17 year old young man with severe brain damage. His behavior, readiness skills, adaptive skills, as well as academic skills are developed at the similar level as those of a 7 year old boy. If we were to pick goals that were age-appropriate, Peter would be working at a level that was too advanced, if he could even comprehend what was being presented to him. Providing him assignments, projects and instruction at his developmental age (7 year old) would give him tasks that he would at least have a chance of being successful at.

Knowing the Current Level of Performance of any student not only guides educators which curricular outcomes or standards to use, it also assists educators with selecting topics, strategies, as well as assessments that are appropriate for the students.

Therefore, before selecting any goal, make sure you know the following:

1. Which executive function do you want to work on?
2. What can the student demonstrate to you (current level of performance)?
3. How does the student learn best?

Keeping track of these three mandatories help you select goals to assist in meeting a student's needs, rather than selecting needs that fit a goal.

Building Response Inhibition

Dawson and Guare refer to Response Inhibition as "the capacity to think before you act—to resist the urge to say or do something before you've had a chance to evaluate the situation" (2009, p. 187). In classrooms, students who struggle with this skill tend to speak before their turn, do before they think, or even run before placing feet on the floor.

The goals and objectives below address many skills and routines that assist students with creating response inhibition that not only help them become better self-managers, but also accelerate learning and achieving.

1. By June, Student will raise his/her hand at appropriate times during instructional and non-instructional time 90% of the time on 4 out of 5 trials, as documented in Student's log.

2. By June, Student will independently identify and demonstrate a list of 8 different strategies one may use when they are feeling angry or upset in class, with 85% accuracy in 4 out of 5 trials, as documented in Student's log.

3. By June, Student will express his opinion or idea politely and independently in group discussion after listening to other classmates' ideas or opinions, at least 4 out of 5 times with 80% accuracy, as documented in Student's log.

4. By June, Student will independently identify his own frustration level using a Likert Scale 80% of the time, in 4 out of 5 trials, as documented in Student's log.

5. By June, Student will express his opinion or idea politely and independently in group discussion after listening to other classmates' ideas or opinions, at least 4 out of 5 times with 80% accuracy, as documented in Student's log.

6. By June, Student will independently use an appropriate tone of voice when talking with other peers or adults in class, 9 out of 10 times in 4 out of 5 trials, as documented in Student's log.

7. By June, Student will independently wait for the teacher to call his/her name before speaking out in class 80% of the time on 4 of 5 consecutive days, as documented in Student's log.

8. By June, Student will, when not able to convey a message orally, independently take a self-time out so that he/she can write on a piece of paper a word or phrase describing

what message he/she wishes to convey and present it to the interested party, at least 70% of the time, in 4 of 5 situations, as documented in Student's log.

9. By June, after hearing an Educational assistant/teacher give a verbal cue to "stop" "use words slow", Student will independently stop chattering and use a minimum of 1 real word with 90% accuracy in 4 out of 5 days, as documented in Student's log.

10. By June, when given a conflict scenario (see attached listing of conflict scenarios), Student will present effective steps toward a peaceful resolution process, as outlined on a conflict resolution checklist, 60 % of the time in 4 out of 5 trials, as documented in Student's log.

11. By June, Student will do the follow conversational conventions of: maintaining eye contact, staying on topic, asking relevant questions, answering questions accurately, and ending a conversation appropriately, with prompting only if needed, at least 70% of the time in 4 out of 5 trials, as documented in the Student's data log.

12. By June, Student will independently turn his/her head and eyes toward the speaker when directly spoken to, 80% of the time on 4/5 trials, as documented in Student's log.

13. By June, Student will independently "talk with a soft voice" when interacting with other staff or Students during the school day, 70% of the time in 4 out of 5 situations, as documented in Student's log.

14. By June, Student will successfully respond to teacher and educational assistants request to follow the rules in the classroom, prior to a third warning, on 8 out of 10 trials with 90% accuracy, as documented on Student's log.

Improving Emotional Control

In Smart but Scattered, the authors define Emotional Control as "the ability to manage emotions to achieve goals, complete tasks, or control and direct your behavior" (Dawson & Guare, 2009, p. 205). Students with a healthy emotional control can deal with poor grades, sudden changes in schedules, and manage feelings of anxiety, downheartedness, frustration, and dissatisfaction.

One factor that has been indicated to interfere with emotional control is the inability to effectively express wants and needs, as well as feelings that interfere with learning. Assisting students with improving emotional control can result in less tantrums, less disappointment, increased readiness for learning, and a noticeable increase in enjoying school. Below are examples of goals and objectives to assist students in developing healthy emotional responses.

15. By June, Student will independently identify when he/she is experiencing high anxiety and signal the teacher or educational assistant for support, 90% of the time in 4 out of 5 trials, as documented in Student's log.

16. By June, Student will independently practice restraint (see attached sheet) in responding to negative situations, 85% of the time in 9 out of 10 trials, as documented in Student's log.

17. By June, with the assistance of an Educational assistant, Student will name the emotions: happy, sad, excited, afraid, surprised, and angry, from face cards with an accuracy of 75% in 3 out of 4 trials, as documented in Student's log.

18. By June, Student will match PECS® symbols with his/her basic wants and needs (food, drink, bathroom, toy, color, etc.), with minimal assistance 4 out of 5 times over a 2 week trial, as documented in Student's log.

19. By June, Student will independently choose from a list of self-control techniques displayed on the inside of his binder (either taking 3 deep breaths, counting to 5, thinking calm thoughts or going for a walk) , and follow one of these techniques 90% of the time, in 4 out of 5 trials, as documented in Student's log.

20. By June, Student will demonstrate peer level social skills (see attached sheet) with a group of classmates through a cooperative board game, designed to be played by teams competing against each other, with 80% accuracy in 3 out of 4 trials, as documented in Student's log.

21. By June, Student will, with minimal supervision from the classroom teacher and educational assistant, participate in an academic group activity in the classroom, using turn taking and using peer-level language, for a 30 minute period, with an 80% success rate, in 4 out of 5 trials, as documented in Student's log.

22. By June, without support, Student, when experiencing difficulty on a learning task, will follow a basic 3 step problem solving procedure (please see attached steps), and be respectful with his/her teacher, educational assistant, and classmates, 80% of the time, in 7 out of 10 trials, as documented in Student's log.

23. By June, Student , with fidelity and educational assistant prompting, will have at least one positive, independent social interaction with a peer buddy, during the school day, for at least 10 minutes a day over 8 of 10 days, as documented in Student's log.

24. By June, with limited visual prompts, Student will match 12 core emotions (frustrated, calm, embarrassed, excited, scared, happy, lonely, nervous, confused, sad, surprised, angry) with facial expressions, and briefly describe these 12 core emotions, with 90% accuracy in 4 of 5 trials, as documented in Student's log.

25. By June, when participating in class discussions, Student will independently speak in a voice loud enough for the class to hear, 4 out of 5 times on 4 out of 5 days, as documented in Student's log.

26. By June, with frequent prompting, Student will select and use stress reducing strategies, in order to promote positive mental health, 80% of the time in 8 out of 10 trials, as documented in Student's log.

27. By June, with occasional prompts, Student will leave the classroom to calm down in a pre-arranged space, when feeling frustrated in class, 80% of the time in 4 out of 5 trials, as documented in Student's log

28. By the end of June, Student will independently determine what response shows empathy by responding in a caring manner when someone is hurt or upset, with 90% accuracy in 9 out of 10 situations, as documented in Student's log.

29. By June, with verbal support, Student will use appropriate replacement behaviors (see attached sheet), when expressing anger or frustration, 90% of the time in 4 out of 5 situations, as documented in Student's log.

30. By June, with verbal reminders from an Educational assistant, Student will circle 4 out of 7 good personal care practices listed in the "Developing Independence in Personal Care Checklist, with at least 60% accuracy in 3 out of 5 trials, as documented in Student's log.

31. By June, Student will independently say "no, this is dangerous", using pictures as guides when asked to do something dangerous in a role play situation with a minimum of 2 of the following 6 people - Student support worker, resource teacher, principal, classroom teacher, educational assistant, or unfamiliar teacher, 90% of the time, 4 out of 5 days, as documented in Student's log.

32. By June, when becoming visibly upset, Student will be able to, with educational assistant prompting when needed, choose an effective strategy and calm down within 5 minutes, 90% of the time, in 4 out of five episodes, as recorded in educational assistant's daybook.

33. By June, with limited verbal prompting, Student will keep his/her hands to self and be without incident of assaulting other Students or destroying school property in all situations, 100% of the time 5 of 5 days, as documented in Student's log.

34. By June, with frequent prompts by the teacher or educational assistant, Student will demonstrate the positive social skills of: 1) appropriate use of personal space, 2) avoiding inappropriate touch of others, and 3) not interrupting but taking turn in the conversation, with peers, in the classroom 80% of the time in 4 of 5 reported situations

35. By June, with occasional verbal prompts, Student will use stress reducing strategies (may include but not limited to: self-calming strategies, self-time out safe area in the school, leaving class to talk to school social worker, calling mother or grandparents) 80% in 8 out of 10 situations, as documented in progress assessment results.

36. By June, with encouragement from an Educational assistant, in the classroom, Student will engage in play with various sensory toys with a classmate, a minimum of 10 minutes, 4 out of 5 days.

37. By June, with occasional educational assistant assistance, Student will actively participate in 4 out of 6 self-esteem builder lessons, 90% of the time, 4 out of 5 days, as documented in a Log for Intensive Support.

38. By June, when becoming upset, Student will calm him/herself down, and experience a maximum of 2 outbursts per week, 90% of the time, 4 out of 5 weeks, as recorded in the Student's behavior log.

39. By June, with limited verbal prompting, Student will independently respond appropriately to peer teasing or bullying, by choosing the appropriate choice as follows: 1) stop and count to 5, 2) ignore, 3) verbally express how you feel, 4) give reasons to stop, 100% of the time in 4 out of 5 situations, as documented in assessment results.

40. By June, with limited support, Student will recognize the feelings of frustration and will choose a method from a list below and consistently calm down, at least 80% of the time in 4 out of 5 situations, as documented in Student's behavior log. (List of strategies include: body breaks, time outs, counting to 5, deep breathing, and relaxations techniques).

41. By June, with the assistance of an Educational assistant, Student will develop positive and self-help decision making skills (see attached sheet) with 70% accuracy in 4 out of 5 trials, as documented in Student's log.

42. By June, Student with fidelity and educational assistant prompting, will have at least one positive, hands off, social interaction with a buddy, during the school day, for at least 10 minutes, 4/5 days a week, as documented in progress assessment results.

43. By June, Student will verbally identify her emotional level, with a rationale, on a 5 point scale, at least four out of five days.

44. By June, Student will remain calm (e.g. refrain from crying, yelling, and/or throwing a tantrum) when a perceived problem (e.g. broken pencil, change in routine, argument with peer) arises and will independently use spoken words to attempt to solve the problem within the classroom, playground, and lunchroom environments, on 4 out of 5 consecutive opportunities.

45. By June, during recess or a classroom play activity, when wanting to share an item, Student will verbally request items from peers (e.g. "May I borrow your pencil?" or "May I play with that when you're finished?"), for 4 out of 5 opportunities.

46. By June, Student will create a visual flow chart to show the steps that lead up to an incident at least once on a two week cycle.

Strengthening Sustained Attention & Teaching Task Initiation

47.   By June, Student will perform a non-preferred task prior to performing a preferred task in 4 out of 5 trials with 90% accuracy without supervision, as documented on Student's behavior log.

48.   By June, Student will independently focus on the task at hand, despite unfinished work 80% of the time in 4 out of 5 trials, as documented on Student's work log.

49.   By June, Student with the help of a visual schedule will stay focused on a non-preferred activity for 5 minutes out of 30 minutes with 80% accuracy on 4 out of 5 trials, as documented on Student's behavior log.

50.   By June, Student will independently start a non-preferred activity when asked to do so by the teacher or educational assistant on the first request 80% of the time on 4 out of 5 trials without prompting, as documented on Student's behavior log.

51.   By June, Student will play a computer game for 10 minutes independently approximately 80% of the time on 4 out of 5 trials, as documented on Student's behavior log.

52.   By June, Student will work at an independent level for 30 consecutive minutes followed by a 10 minute body break, with little supervision from an Educational Assistant or teacher, 80% of the time, 4 out of 5 classes, as documented on Student's log.

53.   By June, Student will work independently for 5 minutes on a teacher directed task with 80% success rate in 8 out of 10 trials over a 2 week period, as documented on Student's log.

54.   By June, Student will consistently work for 20 minutes with the direct help of a teacher or educational assistant (assisted learning) (using a countdown timer) on assignments, 100% of the time, on 5 out of 5 trials, as documented on Student's log.

55.   By June, Student will independently work on preferred academic tasks for 10 minutes in 4 out of 5 trials, with 80 % accuracy, as documented on Student's log.

56.   By June, Student will (with limited supervision) complete one 20 minute seatwork assignment in each of his/her classes for a full day, in 4 out of 5 trials with 80% accuracy, as documented on Student's log.

57.   Student will, with the assistance of a desk legend and minimal verbal instructions from the teacher, independently complete a seatwork assignment 8 out of 10 times over a one week period, as documented on Student's log.

58. By June, Student with the support of his educational assistant, will use a 3 minute grace period to meet the preparation requirements for a change in subject areas, and comply successfully in 7 out of 10 trials in a 6 day cycle, as documented on Student's log.

59. By June, without support, Student will remain on task to complete assigned work in class, with 80% accuracy in 6 out of 8 trials, as documented on Student's log.

60. By June, Student will use an effort gauge at the completion of tasks or at the end of the time designated task, and record effort level 80% of the time in 4 of 5 trials, as documented on Student's log.

61. By June, with occasional prompts, Student will complete his/her assignments to the best of his/her ability, through the use of an Effort Gauge 3 out of 5 times in at least 4 out of 5 trials, as documented on Student's log.

62. By June, Student will independently demonstrate at least 3 listening skills when listening to educational assistant or teacher instructions (see attached sheet) with 80% accuracy on 4 out of 5 trials, as documented on Student's log.

63. By June, with verbal reminders from the educational assistant, Student will complete seatwork assignments with at least 60% accuracy in the Seatwork Assignment Checklist in 3 out of 5 trials, as documented on Student's log.

64. By June, Student will independently complete 5 assignments per day, with 5 or less prompts, with 85% accuracy on 4 out of 5 trials, as documented on Student's log.

65. By June, with positive feedback being given intermittently, and minimal prompts, Student will stay on task for a minimum 20 minute period over 4 out of 5 observations, as documented in Student's log.

66. By June, with help of visual, verbal, and physical support, Student will maintain a minimum 5 minute period of being on task in an activity, with 80% accuracy in 4 out of 5 trials, as documented in Student's log.

67. By June, with teacher or educational assistant support, Student will sit for a minimum of 5 minutes and interact with a book by sitting quietly, listening, and pointing at the pictures, when prompted at least 70% of the time in 3 out of 4 trials, as documented in Student's log.

68. By June, with a maximum of one prompt from the teacher or educational assistant, Student will pay attention for at least 15 minutes at a time, in 4 out of 5 observations, as documented in Student's log.

69. By June, with limited support, Student will independently demonstrate "on task" behavior for a minimum of 10 minutes, when engaged in a non-preferred task in 4 of 5 classes, as documented in Student's log.

70. By June, Student will stay in the regular classroom and engage in an individual activity (see attached sheet) for at least 10 minutes per period for 3 out of 5 periods per day over 4 to 5 consecutive days, as documented in Student's log.

71. By June, Student will hold his/her toothbrush, hand over hand, and brush his/her teeth for a maximum of 2 minutes at least 60% of the time in 2 out of 4 trials, as documented in Student's log.

72. By June, Student will stay on task, working at his/her desk in the classroom setting, with only 1 verbal reminder from the teacher or educational assistant, for a minimum period of 10 minutes at least 90% of time, in 4 out of 5 occasions, as documented in Student's log.

73. By June, Student will independently continue to work on assigned work in class until directed to stop for recess or other dismissal times by the teacher, 90% of the time on 4 consecutive days out of 5, as documented in progress assessment.

74. By June, during shared reading activities with the class, Student will independently stay on task during class lessons, paying attention and track what is being read, with minimal prompts from a teacher or educational assistant, over a maximum of 30 minute period, 4 out of 5 occasions, as documented in the Student data log.

75. By June, with help of visual and physical supports applied progressively by a teacher or educational assistant, Student will stay focused on an activity in the classroom, for at least a 5 minute period on 4 out of 5 trials.

76. By June, with educational assistant highlighting sections of work as a model, Student will independently use a highlighter to chunk a worksheet assignment into manageable sections, and then copy the section 90% of the time in 4 out of 5 trials as documented in the Student's data log.

77. By June, Student will complete a minimum of 5 non preferred class assignments per day, with 5 or fewer prompts from a teacher or educational assistant, as documented in an Assignment Monitoring Tracking Sheet.

78. By June, in the classroom, Student will independently attend to a task which he/she is capable of doing, for a period of 8 minutes of uninterrupted time at least two times per day 4 out of 5 days, as documented in an Independent Task Tracking sheet.

79. By June, Student will independently maintain an unbroken focus on a non-preferred academic task for a minimum 10 minutes during class time, with 80% accuracy in 4 out of 5 trials, as indicated on the Student's tracking log.

80. By June, Student will play a computer game for a minimum time allotment of 20 minutes, independently without needing a teacher or educational assistant in close proximity, at least 80% of the time in 4 out of 5 trials, as documented in Student's log.

81. By June, Student will maintain a minimum of 10 minutes of on task behavior doing independent work time with minimal educational assistant prompting, on 8 out of 10 trials over a period of a week, as documented in Student's log.

82. By June, Student will independently maintain on task performance on non-preferred academic tasks assigned in the classroom, for a minimum of 15 minutes, with 90% accuracy in 4/5 situations, as documented in progress assessments.

83. By June, the Student will demonstrate the 4 steps to ignoring distractions (as listed), 6 out of 8 periods in a school day for 8/10 consecutive days.

84. By June, the learner will use a positive word selected from a visual chart to describe the events of the day at least four times out of six in a six day cycle.

85. By June, Student will say "excuse me" and wait for a social cue in at least 7 out of 10 times before beginning a conversation.

86. By then End of June, when given positive feedback ("You did a good job"), and a verbal cue, ("Remember to be proud of your-self"), the Student will respond with a positive statement such as, ("Thank-you"), in 5 out of 10 interactions.

Promoting, Planning, and Prioritizing & Fostering Organization

87. By June, Student will independently transition, with the help of a visual schedule and be prepared for new subjects 90% of the time on 4 out of 5 days, as documented in Student's log.

88. By June, Student will be successfully cued by a time-timer, and the use of a visual schedule and be prepared for his next class with the correct scribbler, books, etc. with 95% accuracy, in 4 out of 5 trials, as documented in Student's log.

89. By June, Student will manage time independently, so that he/she is able to change from one activity to another on his/her timetable, with 90% accuracy 4 out of 5 consecutive times, as documented in Student's log.

90. By June, when the bell rings for the 5 minute break between classes, Student will manage her time of going to his/her locker, washroom, or drinking fountain, and move to class and be sitting at his/her desk, when the bell rings to start class, 2 out of 3 times per day over a week period 100% of the time, as documented in Student's log.

91. By June 2010, when provided with a 3 minute warning using a visual schedule, Student will follow the direction to change activities in the classroom setting, at least 8 out of 10 times 4 out of 5 consecutive days, as documented in Student's log.

92. By June, Student will independently begin a newly presented activity in class, with minimal prompting, and stay on task for a minimum of 5 minutes without prompting, with 90% accuracy in 4 out of 5 trials, as documented in Student's log.

93. By June, Student will, when the bell rings, independently gather his/her things from that period and put them away, and get the books and supplies out for the next class period, prior to the start of a lesson, with 80% success rate over 5 days of classes, as documented in Student's log.

94. By June, Student will with educational assistant assistance, will at the end of the day, be ready (getting outside cloths on, homework etc.) and wait outside 5 minutes, early in preparation for the school bus to pick him/her up for home time, with 100% accuracy in 5 out of 5 trials, as documented in Student's log.

95. By June, with occasional prompts and the use a visual timer, Student will review and follow a set of expectations for each transition period in school with 80% accuracy in 5 of 5 trials, as documented in Student's log.

96. By June, when provided with a 2 minute warning, using a picture schedule, Student will follow the required directions to prepare for satellite classes, 90% of the time, in at least 4 out of 5 consecutive days, as documented in Student's log.

97. By June, Student will independently return to class after using the bathroom, within 2 minutes after leaving class, 90% of the time, 4 out of 5 days, as documented in Student's log.

98. By June, with the aid of a visual timer and educational assistant support, Student will put away work from previous assignments and start new assignments within 3 minutes in 6 periods of 8, over a 3-5 day period, 90% of the time, as documented in Student's log.

99. By June, in the classroom, using a timer and visual prompting, Student will be able to, after a 5 minute advanced warning, put away an activity, and get ready for the next activity within 1 minute, 80% of the time in 4 out of 5 trials, as documented in Student's log.

100. By June, Student will independently retell instructions to educational assistant, with 90% accuracy, 4 out of 5 days, as documented in Student's log.

101. By June, with verbal reminders from an Educational assistant, Student will remember needed supplies i.e. a pencil, proper scribbler, required texts, and other supplies, 80% of the time in 3 out of 5 trials, as documented in Student's log.

102. By June, when a change has been made to the daily schedule, Student will use self-talk 60% of the time, to calm down and accept the change within a 2 minute period, in 4 out of 5 instances, as recorded in an Educational assistant's day planner.

103. By June, with limited support, and using a visual timer and cueing system, Student will take no longer than 5 minutes to transition from one task to a complete other task, with 90% accuracy, 4 out of 5 times, as documented in Student's log.

104. By June, Student will, with visual supports, follow a change in routine (by listening to the instruction and asking for clarification if needed) and follow the instruction of the teacher or educational assistant, at least 80% of the time, as documented in the Student's data log.

105. By June, Student will, at recess on the playground, with advanced warning and picture support, come in to the school after the bell, within a 2 minute time period, at least 90% of the time, unassisted in 4 out of 5 trials, as documented in Student's log.

106. By June, Student will transition from a wheelchair to mat to standing on a table lift, without fussing, 90% of the time in 4 out of 5 trials, as documented in Student's log.

107. By June, independently, Student will remain on task in the classroom, when completing non preferred work, for minimum 10 minute duration, 80% of the time in 4 of 5 school periods, over 4 to 5 days, as documented in Student's log.

108. By June, with fidelity, and the supervision of an Educational assistant or teacher, Student will walk in a line with their classmates to class at an appropriate pace, without incident, 100% of the time in 5 out of 5 trials, as documented in Student's log.

109. By the end of June, the Student will with verbal cue gaze at an object/choice for at least three seconds in 4/5 trials.

110. By the end of June, Student will, when shown the clean-up picture, with adult assistance (hand-holding), walk away from children, go to an area to clean up, putting away at least four toys from ground/table anywhere on the shelf, at least three out of four days a week.

111. By June, when provided with physical assistance, a verbal prompt "Gym time. Gym time finished." and a visual schedule showing up to 3 photos indicating Gym, Computer and Snack time, the Student will follow the direction to switch and attend to each activity at least 80 % of the time.

112. By June, the Student will stay in his seat with his 'body still' (feet on the floor, bum on the seat, sitting erect, and hands still on the table) during oral instruction given by the teacher in the regular classroom for at least 3 minutes in 3 out of 5 trials.

113. The Student will work without stopping until his scheduled break, with visual prompting when necessary, at least 4 out of 5 checks, by the end of June.

114. By June, during a 3-minute conversation with another individual, Student will appropriately respond (e.g. stay on topic, speak in turn, not interrupt) and elaborate (e.g. asking on-topic questions and replying to previous comments) on the topic being discussed during 4 out of 5 opportunities.

115. By June, Student will transition from one scheduled academic activity to the next scheduled academic activity (preferred or not) within (10 seconds) of being given a signal or directive (e.g. a bell rung, or the teacher singing a transition song), without showing maladaptive behaviors (e.g. crying, arguing, throwing a tantrum, noncompliance), during 4 out of 5 opportunities.

116. By June, Student will have increased awareness of objects within and outside of personal space 95% of the time.

117. By June, Student, with prompting and in 4/5 trials, will acknowledge (e.g. by pointing) the picture of the next activity on his visual schedule when presented with that picture.

118. By June, Student with direction and guidance, will use a checklist to demonstrate daily good hygiene practices including personal grooming and use of necessary personal hygiene products in 6/8 trials with 90% accuracy.

119. By June, Student will list and find specific local landmarks in the school/community area, as chosen by his teacher, he could use to locate himself (if lost) in 5/5 trials with 80% accuracy.

120. By June, Student will independently connect an iPad to a Light Speed Red Cat (Sound Amplifying system) to convey a message to the rest of the students 80% of time.

121. By June, Student will indicate to the teacher the need to go to the washroom by displaying a washroom symbol on the iPad 100% of time.

Cultivating Metacognition

Metacognition is referred to as the ability to problem solve, self-monitor, self-evaluate, and sometimes self-regulate. Others have included in metacognition various refection skills, as well strategies to analyses facts.

122. By the end of June, Student will independently and accurately match the oral names of animals (bear, moose, fish, deer, bird), food (apple, toast, cereal, sandwich, pizza, potatoes), and primary colors by pointing to the appropriate pictures, when displaced in a group of no less than 4 pictures, 75% of the time in 4 out of 5 trials, as documented in Student's log.

123. By June, Student will independently create and manage a weekly budget of $20, and be within $2 more or less of a target, with 80% accuracy in 4 out of 5 trials, as documented in Student's progress assessment.

124. By June, Student will independently prepare a recipe with 6 simple ingredients from start to finish, in four out of five trials with 90% accuracy, as documented in Student's progress assessment.

125. By June, when given 15 basic commands using prepositions, Student will correctly follow these commands with no visual cues or help from his teacher with 90% accuracy in 4 out of 5 trials, as documented in Student's progress assessment.

126. By June, Student will independently compose and write an 8 sentence journal entry, reflecting on the day, with 80 % accuracy in 4 out of 5 journal entries, as documented in Student's progress assessment.

127. By June, using a light box activity, Student will correctly match 2 picture cards from a choice of 4 picture cards by identifying similar characteristics (attributes) with 85% accuracy in 8 out of 10 trials, as documented in Student's progress assessment.

128. By the end of June, Student will independently edit his/her writing, so that he/she has no more than 2 errors in each of the following categories (run on sentences, capitalization) on 4 out of 5 written assignments, as documented in Student's progress assessment.

129. By June, Student will independently use a self-editing checklist (see attachment) when reviewing written assignments at least 80% of the time in 4 out of 5 trials, as documented in progress assessment results.

130. By June, with educational assistant prompting only when needed, Student will determine which tool/strategy would best help him/her complete a math problem, then successfully utilize the appropriate tool/strategy to complete the math problem, 80% of the time in 4 out of 5 trials, as documented in Student's progress assessment.

131. By June, Student will independently identify the importance of taking his medications and list the possible side effect of his medication, in 4 out of 5 trials, with 90% accuracy, as documented in Student's log.

132. By June, using 10 facial expression pictures, Student will indicate to the teacher which feelings are indicated in each of the pictures and how they relate to self, with 70% accuracy in 4 out of 5 trials, as documented in Student's log.

==O==

About the Author

Chris de Feyter grew up in Europe, where he earned a Bachelor degree in education, as well as Master degree in special education and psychology. In 2012, he earned a second Master Degree in Education, and recently completed his doctoral degree program.

Next to working in elementary and secondary schools, Chris managed several psychology practices, focusing on learning disabilities, anxiety, and depression. In that capacity, he appeared on several national and international talk shows and news channels. Currently, Chris works for a large school division in Canada, where he focuses on students with diverse, intensive, and special needs.

Consultation & Helpdesk

Please visit Chris' professional website to receive complimentary SMART Goal updates. The website also provides opportunities to connect to Chris to ask questions about goals and strategies.

http://CDFResearch.com

Other Publications

800+ Measurable IEP Goals and Objectives for Use in K-12 Classrooms

800+ Measurable IEP Goals and Objectives

For use in K - 12 and in Home School Settings

CHRIS DE FEYTER EdD

Made in the USA
Lexington, KY
21 September 2015